The princess and the baby

Story by Penny Frank

Illustrated by Tony Morris

Guideposts

9

CARMEL • NEW YORK 10512

The Bible tells us how God chose the Israelites to be his special people. He made them a promise that he would always love and care for them. But they must obey him.

The Israelites had first come from Canaan to Egypt to find food. Joseph had saved them from starving to death. This story happens after Joseph has died. The Israelites have become slaves to the Egyptians. You can find the story in your Bible in Exodus, chapters 1 and 2.

Copyright © 1984 Lion Publishing

Published by
Lion Publishing plc
Icknield Way, Tring, Herts, England
Lion Publishing Corporation
1705 Hubbard Avenue, Batavia,
Illinois 60510, USA
Albatross Books Pty Ltd
PO Box 320, Sutherland, NSW 2232, Australia

First edition 1984
Reprinted 1984, 1985, 1986, 1987

Printed and bound in Hong Kong by Mandarin Offset Marketing (HK) Ltd
This Guideposts edition is published by special arrangement with Lion Publishing

British Library Cataloguing in Publication Data
Frank, Penny
The princess and the baby. – (The Lion Story Bible; 9)
1. Moses *(Prophet)* – Juvenile literature
I. Title   II. Morris, Tony
222'.120924   BS580.M6

Library of Congress Cataloging in Publication Data
1. Moses (Biblical leader)—Juvenile literature. 2. Bible. O.T.—Biography–Juvenile literature. [1. Moses (Biblical leader) 2. Bible stories—O.T.] I. Morris, Tony, ill. II. Title. III. Series: Frank, Penny. Lion Story Bible; 9.
BS580.M6F67 1984   222'.1209505
84-17120

There were many Israelites living in the land of Egypt. It was not their own country.

The Egyptians looked at the Israelites who lived in their country and said, 'There are so many of them. They will soon be taking over Egypt!'

There was a new king in Egypt. He looked at all the Israelites and said, 'Something must be done. There are too many of them. They might fight us and turn us out of our own land.'

'They are useful slaves, but we must think of a way to make them tired and weak so that they cannot fight as soldiers.'

So the king of Egypt made the
Israelites work very hard.

They had to start early in the
morning. They went back to their
homes when it was late at night.

The Israelites had to make bricks for the Egyptian cities. They had to do all the hard work on the farms too.

They became hot and tired. But they were still stronger than the Egyptians.

The Egyptians were afraid of them.

'I have a good idea,' said the king.
'We will kill all their baby boys when
they are born. Soon they will have no
young men to fight us.'

8

So the king of Egypt told the people, 'All the Israelite baby boys must be killed.'

The Israelites were very sad. They loved their baby boys. They wanted them to grow up to be strong young men.

One Israelite woman who had a baby boy said to her little girl, Miriam, 'I can't let them kill him. I want to watch him grow up. I love him so much.'

So she made a tiny floating cradle for him and put it on the river among the reeds.

Every day they put him in his special hiding place. His sister Miriam sat on the river bank and watched.

One day Miriam saw the king's
daughter walking beside the river.
She had some servants with her.

Miriam did not know what to do, and
there was no time to fetch her mother.

'What's that?' asked the princess,
pointing to the tiny floating cradle.

They pulled the cradle to the river
bank, opened the lid and looked inside.
There was the little baby.

He was crying. But when he saw the
princess he put out his hands to touch
her face.

'What a lovely baby,' said the princess.
'He is an Israelite. I wish I had
someone to look after him. Then I could
keep him.'

Then Miriam came down the bank to the path. 'I know someone who would look after him for you,' she said. 'I'll just go and get her.'

Miriam ran to get her mother. The princess did not know that she was the baby's own mother.

'Please look after him,' said the princess to the baby's mother. 'When he is old enough he can come and live at my palace. I shall call him Moses.'

Miriam and her mother were so happy
to have the baby boy back.

No one could kill him now, because
they knew that Moses belonged to the
princess.

18

Every day the little family watched
Moses grow. He learned to walk and
talk. He laughed and played with
Miriam by the river.

When Moses was old enough he went
to live at the palace with the princess.
He grew up as a rich young man.

He knew he was not an Egyptian. He often saw the Israelites as they worked at the palace. He saw how tired and sad they were.

'I wish I could help them,' he said.

God had not forgotten the Israelites. He knew they needed a strong leader to take them away from Egypt.

God wanted them to go back to the land of Canaan.

'I will give Moses the job of leading the Israelites out of Egypt,' said God. 'And I will be with him just as I was with Joseph.'

But that is another story.

The Story Bible Series from Guideposts is made up of 50 individual stories for young readers, building up an understanding of the Bible as one story—God's story—a story for all time and all people.

The Old Testament story books tell the story of a great nation—God's chosen people, the Israelites—and God's love and care for them through good times and bad. The stories are about people who knew and trusted God. From this nation came one special person, Jesus Christ, sent by God to save all people everywhere.

The New Testament story books cover the life and teaching of God's Son, Jesus. The stories are about the people he met, what he did and what he said. Almost all we know about the life of Jesus is recorded in the four Gospels—Matthew, Mark, Luke and John. The word gospel means 'good news.'

The last four stories in this section are about the first Christians, who started to tell others the 'good news,' as Jesus had commanded them—a story which continues today all over the world.

The story of *The princess and the baby* comes from the second book of the Bible, Exodus chapters 1 and 2. The Israelites were slaves in Egypt, toiling to supply their quotas of bricks for the king of Egypt's great buildings. Because of their numbers they were a potential threat to the nation's security, so the king decreed that at birth every boy baby was to be thrown into the River Nile and drowned. But Miriam's little brother, the baby born to Jochebed and her husband, was special. God had chosen him to lead his people out of Egypt. And so, through a mother's love, and the smile of a baby which moved the princess's heart, Moses was saved.